Sing A Song Of Christmas

Mary Thompson

Illustrated by David Meldrum

Chester Music Limited

(A division of Music Sales Ltd.)
8/9 Frith Street, London W1V 5TZ

Contents

Cover design by Chloë Alexander
Printed and bound in the United Kingdom by
Caligraving Limited, Thetford, Norfolk.

Order No. CH61495   ISBN 0-7119-7530-2

I Saw Three Ships

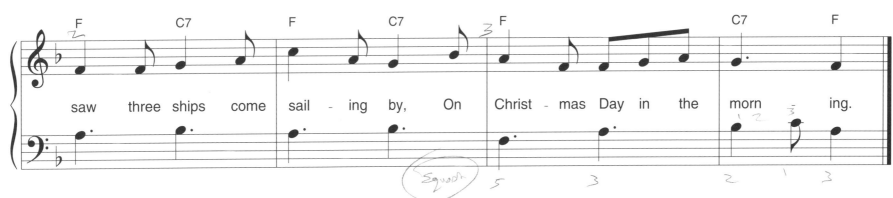

1. I saw three ships come sailing by,
   On Christmas Day, on Christmas Day,
   I saw three ships come sailing by,
   On Christmas Day in the morning.

2. And what was in those ships all three?
   On Christmas Day, on Christmas Day,
   And what was in those ships all three?
   On Christmas Day in the morning.

3. Our Saviour Christ and His lady.
   On Christmas Day, on Christmas Day.
   Our Saviour Christ and His lady.
   On Christmas Day in the morning.

We Three Kings Of Orient Are

1.   We three Kings of Orient are;
     Bearing gifts we travel so far,
     Field and fountain, moor and mountain,
     Following yonder star:

O star of wonder, star of night,
Star with royal beauty bright,
Westward leading, still proceeding,
Guide us to thy perfect light.

2. Born a King on Bethlehem plain,
    Gold I bring, to crown Him again,
    King for ever, ceasing never,
    Over us all to reign:

    O star of wonder...

3. Frankincense to offer have I;
    Incense owns a Deity nigh:
    Prayer and praising, all men raising,
    Worship Him, God most high:

    O star of wonder...

If you want to do a nativity play, verses 2, 3 and 4 can be sung as solos, by the three Kings.

4. Myrrh is mine; its bitter perfume
    Breathes a life of gathering gloom;
    Sorrowing, sighing, bleeding, dying,
    Sealed in the stone-cold tomb:

    O star of wonder...

5. Glorious now, behold Him arise,
    King, and God, and sacrifice!
    Alleluia, Alleluis;
    Earth to the heavens replies:

    O star of wonder...

Once In Royal David's City

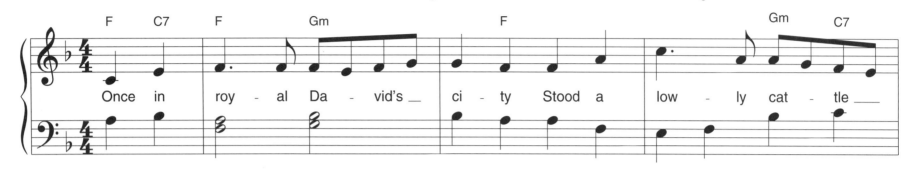

Once in roy - al Da - vid's __ ci - ty Stood a low - ly cat - tle __

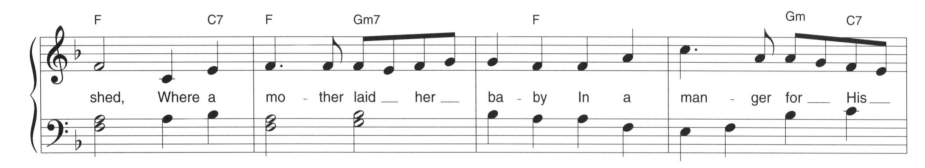

shed, Where a mo - ther laid __ her __ ba - by In a man - ger for __ His __

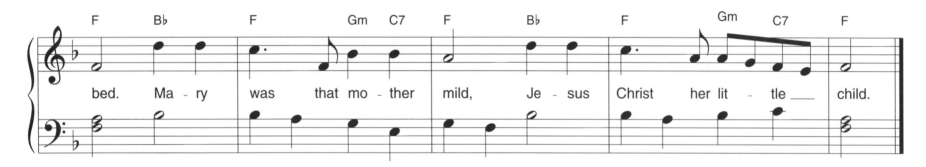

bed. Ma - ry was that mo - ther mild, Je - sus Christ her lit - tle __ child.

1.   Once in royal David's city
Stood a lowly cattle shed,
Where a mother laid her baby
In a manger for his bed.
Mary was that mother mild,
Jesus Christ her little child.

2. He came down to earth from heaven
Who is God and Lord of all,
And His shelter was a stable,
And His cradle was a stall;
With the poor and mean and lowly
Lived on earth our Saviour Holy.

3. And through all His wondrous childhood
He would honour and obey,
Love and watch the lowly maiden,
In whose gentle arms He lay.
Christian children all must be
Mild, obedient, good as He.

4. For He is our childhood's pattern,
Day by day like us He grew,
He was little, weak and helpless,
Tears and smiles like us He knew.
And He feeleth for our sadness,
And He shareth in our gladness.

5. And our eyes at last shall see Him,
Through His own redeeming love,
For that child so dear and gentle
Is our Lord in heaven above;
And He leads his children on
To the place where He is gone.

6. Not in that poor lowly stable,
With the oxen standing by,
We shall see Him, but in heaven,
Set at God's right hand on high,
Where like stars His children crowned
All in white shall wait around.

David's city is another name for Bethlehem.

Away In A Manger

1.   Away in a manger, no crib for a bed,
The little Lord Jesus lay down His sweet head.
The stars in the bright sky looked down where He lay,
The little Lord Jesus asleep on the hay.

2.   The cattle are lowing, the baby awakes,
But little Lord Jesus, no crying He makes.
I love Thee Lord Jesus! Look down from the sky,
And stay by my side until morning is nigh.

3.   Be near me Lord Jesus; I ask Thee to stay
Close by me for ever, and love me, I pray.
Bless all the dear children in Thy tender care,
And fit us for heaven, to live with Thee there.

Deck The Hall

Deck the hall with boughs of hol-ly, Fa la la la la, la la la la,

'Tis the sea-son to be jol-ly, Fa la la la la, la la la la,

Don we now our gay ap-pa-rel, Fa la la, la la la, la la la,

Troll the an-cient Yule-tide car-ol, Fa la la la la, la la la la.

1. Deck the hall with boughs of holly,
    Fa la la la la, la la la la,
    'Tis the season to be jolly,
    Fa la la la la, la la la la,
    Don we now our gay apparel,
    Fa la la, la la la, la la la,
    Troll the ancient Yuletide carol,
    Fa la la la la, la la la la.

2. See the blazing Yule before us,
    Fa la la la la, la la la la,
    Strike the harp and join the chorus,
    Fa la la la la, la la la la,
    Follow me in merry measure,
    Fa la la, la la la, la la la,
    While I tell of Yuletide treasure,
    Fa la la la la, la la la la.

3. Fast away the old year passes,
    Fa la la la la, la la la la,
    Hail the new, ye lads and lasses,
    Fa la la la la, la la la la,
    Sing we joyous all together,
    Fa la la, la la la, la la la,
    Heedless of the wind and weather,
    Fa la la la la, la la la la.

The First Nowell

1.
The first Nowell the angel did say,
Was to certain poor shepherds in fields as they lay;
In fields where they lay keeping their sheep,
On a cold winter's night that was so deep.

Nowell, Nowell, Nowell, Nowell,
Born is the King of Israel.

2.
They lookèd up and saw a star,
Shining in the east, beyond them far,
And to the earth it gave great light,
And so it continued both day and night.

Nowell, Nowell, Nowell, Nowell...

3.
And by the light of that same star,
Three wise men came from country far;
To seek for a King was their intent,
And to follow the star wherever it went.

Nowell, Nowell, Nowell, Nowell...

4. This star drew nigh unto the north-west,
O'er Bethlehem it took to rest,
And there it did both stop and stay,
Right over the place where Jesus lay.

Nowell, Nowell, Nowell, Nowell...

5. Then entered in those wise men three,
Full reverently upon their knee,
And offered there, in His presence,
Their gold and myrrh and frankincense.

Nowell, Nowell, Nowell, Nowell...

6.
Then let us all with one accord,
Sing praises to our heavenly Lord,
That hath made heaven and earth of nought,
And with His blood mankind hath bought.

Nowell, Nowell, Nowell, Nowell...

God Rest You Merry Gentlemen

1. God rest you merry gentlemen,
    Let nothing you dismay,
    For Jesus Christ our Saviour
    Was born on Christmas Day;
    To save us all from Satan's power
    When we were gone astray:

    O tidings of comfort and joy,
    Comfort and joy,
    O tidings of comfort and joy.

2. From God, our heavenly Father,
    A blessèd angel came,
    And unto certain shepherds
    Brought tidings of the same,
    That there was born in Bethlehem
    The Son of God by name:

    O tidings of comfort and joy...

3. The shepherds at those tidings
    Rejoicèd much in mind,
    And left their flocks a-feeding,
    In tempest, storm and wind,
    And went to Bethlehem straightaway
    This blessèd babe to find:

    O tidings of comfort and joy...

4. But when to Bethlehem they came,
    Whereat this infant lay,
    They found Him in a manger,
    Where oxen feed on hay;
    His mother Mary kneeling,
    Unto the Lord did pray:

    O tidings of comfort and joy...

5. Now to the Lord sing praises,
    All you within this place,
    And with true love and brotherhood
    Each other now embrace;
    This holy tide of Christmas
    All others doth deface:

    O tidings of comfort and joy...

God rest you merry gentlemen means "May God keep everyone happy".

Silent Night

1.   Silent night, holy night,
      All is calm, all is bright,
      Round yon virgin, mother and child,
      Holy infant so tender and mild,
      Sleep in heavenly peace,
      Sleep in heavenly peace.

This carol comes from Germany.

2.   Silent night, holy night,
      Shepherds wake at the sight;
      Glory streams from heaven afar,
      Heavenly hosts sing Alleluia.
      Christ the Saviour is born!
      Christ the Saviour is born!

3.   Silent night, holy night,
      Son of God, love's pure light;
      Radiance beams from Thy holy face,
      With the dawn of redeeming grace,
      Jesus, Lord at Thy birth,
      Jesus, Lord at Thy birth.

It Came Upon A Midnight Clear

1. It came upon a midnight clear,
    That glorious song of old,
    From angels bending near the earth,
    To touch their harps of gold:
    "Peace on the earth, good will to men,
    From heav'n's all-gracious King!"
    The world in solemn stillness lay
    To hear the angels sing.

2. Still through the cloven skies they come,
    With peaceful wings unfurled,
    And still their heav'nly music floats
    O'er all the weary world;
    Above its sad and lowly plains
    They bend on heav'nly wing,
    And ever o'er its Babel-sounds
    The blessèd angels sing.

3. Yet with the woes of sin and strife,
    The world has suffered long;
    Beneath the angel-strain have rolled
    Two thousand years of wrong;
    And man, at war with man, hears not
    The love-song which they bring;
    Oh, hush the noise, ye men of strife,
    And hear the angels sing!

4. For lo! The days are hastening on,
    By prophet-bards foretold,
    When with the ever-circling years
    Comes round the age of gold:
    When peace shall over all the earth
    Its ancient splendours fling,
    And the whole world send back the song
    Which now the angels sing.

Try to sing this carol as sweetly as you can.

Il Est Né Le Divin Enfant

Il est né le divin enfant,
Jouez hautbois, résonnez musettes,
Il est né le divin enfant,
Chantons tous son avènement.

This carol comes from France. The title means "The divine child is born".

De puis plus du qua -tre mille ans, Nous le pro -met-taient les pro -phè -tes,

De puis plus de qua -tre mille ans, Nous at -tend -ions cet heu -reux temps.

D.C. al Fine

1. De puis plus de quatre mille ans,
   Nous le promettaient les prophètes,
   De puis plus de quatre mille ans,
   Nous attendions cet heureux temps.

   Il est né le divin enfant...

2. Une étable est son logement,
   Un peu de paille est sa couchette;
   Une étable est son logement,
   Pour un Dieu quel abaissement!

   Il est né le divin enfant...

The Rocking Carol

1. Little Jesus, sweetly sleep, do not stir;
   We will lend a coat of fur,
   We will rock you, rock you, rock you,
   We will rock you, rock you, rock you:
   See the fur to keep you warm,
   Snugly round your tiny form.

2. Mary's little baby, sleep, sweetly sleep;
   Sleep in comfort, slumber deep;
   We will rock you, rock you, rock you,
   We will rock you, rock you, rock you:
   We will serve you all we can,
   Darling, darling little man.

Good King Wenceslas

1. Good King Wenceslas looked out
      On the Feast of Stephen,
    When the snow lay round about,
      Deep and crisp and even;
    Brightly shone the moon that night,
      Though the frost was cruel,
    When a poor man came in sight,
      Gathering winter fuel.

2. "Hither, page and stand by me,
      If thou know'st it, telling,
    Yonder peasant, who is he?
      Where and what his dwelling?"
    "Sire, he lives a good league hence,
      Underneath the mountain,
    Right against the forest fence,
      By Saint Agnes' fountain."

3. "Bring me flesh and bring me wine,
      Bring me pine-logs hither:
    Thou and I will see him dine,
      When we bear them thither."
    Page and monarch, forth they went,
      Forth they went together;
    Through the rude wind's wild lament
      And the bitter weather.

4. "Sire, the night is darker now,
      And the wind blows stronger;
    Fails my heart, I know not how;
      I can go no longer."
    "Mark my footsteps, good my page;
      Tread thou in them boldly:
    Thou shalt find the winter's rage
      Freeze thy blood less coldly."

The Feast of Stephen is on Boxing Day.

5. In his master's steps he trod,
      Where the snow lay dinted;
    Heat was in the very sod
      Which the saint had printed.
    Therefore, Christian men, be sure,
      Wealth or rank possessing,
    Ye who now will bless the poor,
      Shall yourselves find blessing.

Jingle Bells

1. Dashing through the snow
In a one-horse open sleigh,
O'er the fields we go,
Laughing all the way;
Bells on bobtail ring,
Making spirits bright;
What fun it is to ride and sing
A sleighing song tonight.

Oh, jingle bells, jingle bells,
Jingle all the way.
Oh what fun it is to ride
In a one-horse open sleigh.
Oh, jingle bells, jingle bells,
Jingle all the way.
Oh what fun it is to ride
In a one-horse open sleigh.

2.   A day or two ago
I thought I'd take a ride
And soon Miss Fannie Bright
Was seated by my side;
The horse was lean and lank,
Misfortune seemed his lot,
He got into a drifted bank
And then we got upsot!

Oh, jingle bells, jingle bells...

See Amid The Winter's Snow

1. See amid the winter's snow,
   Born for us on earth below;
   See the tender Lamb appears,
   Promised from eternal years:

   Hail, thou ever-blessèd morn;
   Hail, redemption's happy dawn;
   Sing through all Jerusalem,
   Christ is born in Bethlehem.

2. Lo, within a manger lies,
   He who built the starry skies
   He who, throned in height sublime,
   Sits amid the cherubim.

   Hail, thou ever-blessèd morn...

3. Say, ye holy shepherds, say,
   What your joyful news today;
   Wherefore have ye left your sheep
   On the lonely mountain steep?

   Hail, thou ever-blessèd morn...

4. "As we watched at dead of night,
   Lo, we saw a wondrous light;
   Angels singing peace on earth,
   Told us of the Saviour's birth."

   Hail, thou ever-blessèd morn...

5. Sacred Infant, all divine,
   What a tender love was thine,
   Thus to come from highest bliss
   Down to such a world as this!

   Hail, thou ever-blessèd morn...

6. Teach, oh teach us, Holy Child,
   By Thy face so meek and mild.
   Teach us to resemble thee
   In Thy sweet humility.

   Hail, thou ever-blessèd morn...

Sing this carol as gently as you can.

While Shepherds Watched

1. While shepherds watched their flocks by night,
All seated on the ground,
The angel of the Lord came down,
And glory shone around.

2. "Fear not," said he; for mighty dread
    Had seized their troubled minds;
    "Glad tidings of great joy I bring
    To you and all mankind."

3. "To you in David's town this day
    Is born of David's line
    A saviour, who is Christ the Lord;
    And this shall be the sign:"

Swathing bands are strips of material, a bit like bandages.

4. "The heavenly Babe you there shall find
    To human view displayed
    All meanly wrapped in swathing bands,
    And in a manger laid."

5. Thus spake the seraph; and forthwith
    Appeared a shining throng
    Of angels praising God, who thus
    Addressed their joyful song:

6. "All glory be to God on high,
    And to the earth be peace;
    Goodwill henceforth from heaven to men
    Begin and never cease."

Ding Dong! Merrily On High

1. Ding dong! Merrily on high, in heaven the bells are ringing,
    Ding dong! Verily the sky is riven with angels singing.

    Gloria, Hosanna in excelsis.
    Gloria, Hosanna in excelsis.

2. And on earth below, below, let steeple bells be swungen,
    And i-o, i-o, i-o, by priest and people sungen.

    Gloria, Hosanna in excelsis...

3. Pray you, dutifully prime your matin chime, you ringers,
    May you beautifully rhyme your eve-time song, you singers.

    Gloria, Hosanna in excelsis...

O Little Town Of Bethlehem

Melody collected by Ralph Vaughan Williams © Oxford University Press 1928. Reproduced by permission.

1. O little town of Bethlehem,
How still we see thee lie.
Above thy deep and dreamless sleep,
The silent stars go by.
Yet in thy dark streets shineth
The everlasting light.
The hopes and fears of all the years
Are met in thee tonight.

2. O morning stars, together
Proclaim thy holy birth.
And praises sing to God the King
And peace to men on earth.
For Christ is born of Mary
And, gathered all above
While mortals sleep, the angels keep
Their watch of wondering love.

3. How silently, how silently,
The wondrous gift is given!
So God imparts to human hearts
The blessings of His heaven.
No ear may hear His coming,
But in this world of sin,
Where meek souls will receive him, still
The dear Christ enters in.

4. O holy child of Bethlehem,
Descend to us we pray,
Cast out our sin, and enter in,
Be born in us today.
We hear the Christmas angels
The great glad tidings tell:
O come to us, abide with us,
Our Lord Emmanuel.

Hark! The Herald Angels Sing

1. Hark! The herald angels sing,
Glory to the new-born King.
Peace on earth, and mercy mild,
God and sinners reconciled.
Joyful, all you nations rise,
Join the triumph of the skies.
With the angelic hosts proclaim,
"Christ is born in Bethlehem."

Hark! The herald angels sing,
"Glory to the new-born King."

Sing the chorus a little louder than the verses.

2. Christ, by highest heaven adored,
Christ, the everlasting Lord,
Late in time behold him come,
Offspring of a Virgin's womb.
Veiled in flesh the Godhead see;
Hail, the Incarnate Deity,
Pleased as man with man to dwell,
Jesus, our Emmanuel!

Hark! The herald angels sing...

3. Hail, the heaven-born Prince of Peace!
Hail, the Son of righteousness!
Light and life to all He brings,
Risen with healing in His wings.
Mild He lays His glory by,
Born that man no more may die,
Born to raise the sons of earth,
Born to give them second birth.

Hark! The herald angels sing...

Angels From The Realms Of Glory

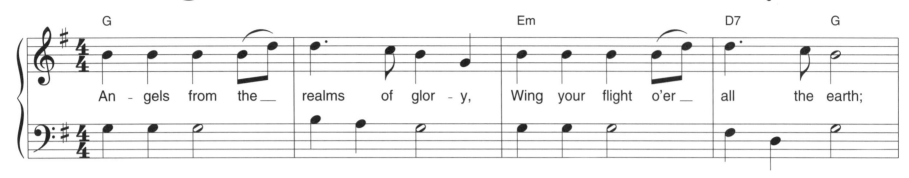

An - gels from the __ realms of glor - y, Wing your flight o'er __ all the earth;

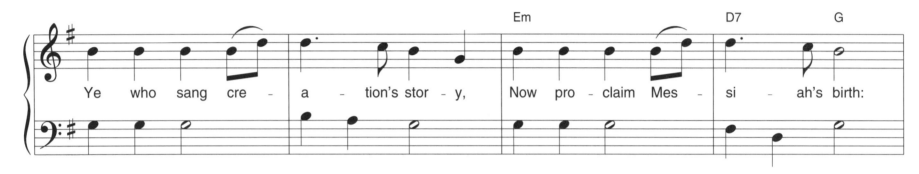

Ye who sang cre - a - tion's stor - y, Now pro - claim Mes - si - ah's birth:

1. Angels from the realms of glory,
    Wing your flight o'er all the earth;
    Ye who sang creation's story,
    Now proclaim Messiah's birth:
    Gloria in excelsis Deo,
    Gloria in excelsis Deo.

2. Shepherds in the fields abiding,
    Watching o'er your flocks by night,
    God with man is now residing;
    Yonder shines the infant Light:
    Gloria in excelsis Deo...

3. Sages, leave your contemplations,
   Brighter visions beam afar;
   Seek the great desire of nations,
   Ye have seen His natal star:
   Gloria in excelsis Deo...

4. Saints before the altar bending,
   Watching long in hope and fear,
   Suddenly the Lord, descending,
   In His temple shall appear:
   Gloria in excelsis Deo...

5. Though an infant now we view Him,
   He shall fill His Father's throne,
   Gather all the nations round Him,
   Every knee shall then bow down:
   Gloria in excelsis Deo...

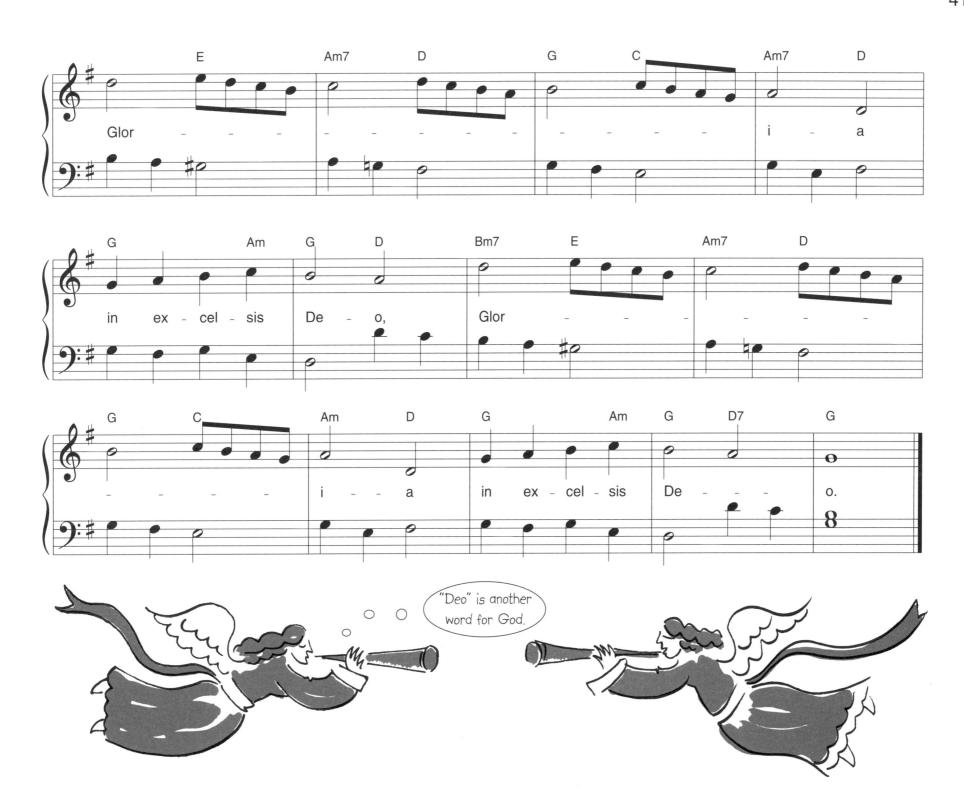

The Holly And The Ivy

1. The holly and the ivy,
   When they are both full grown,
   Of all the trees that are in the wood,
   The holly bears the crown.

   O the rising of the sun,
   And the running of the deer;
   The playing of the merry organ,
   Sweet singing in the choir.

Holly and ivy are often used to make a type of Christmas decoration called a wreath.

2. The holly bears a blossom,
   As white as the lily flower,
   And Mary bore sweet Jesus Christ,
   To be our sweet Saviour:

   O the rising of the sun...

3. The holly bears a berry,
   As red as any blood,
   And Mary bore sweet Jesus Christ,
   To do poor sinners good:

   O the rising of the sun...

4. The holly bears a prickle,
   As sharp as any thorn,
   And Mary bore sweet Jesus Christ,
   On Christmas Day in the morn:

   O the rising of the sun...

5. The holly bears a bark,
   As bitter as any gall,
   And Mary bore sweet Jesus Christ,
   For to redeem us all:

   O the rising of the sun...

O Come, All Ye Faithful

O come, all ye faith - ful, Joy - ful and tri - um - phant, O come ye, O come_____ ye to Beth - - - le hem. Come and be - hold Him, Born the King of An - - gels: O

1. O come, all ye faithful,
   Joyful and triumphant,
   O come ye, o come ye to Bethlehem.
   Come and behold Him,
   Born the King of Angels:

O come let us adore Him,
O come let us adore Him,
O come let us adore Him,
Christ the Lord.

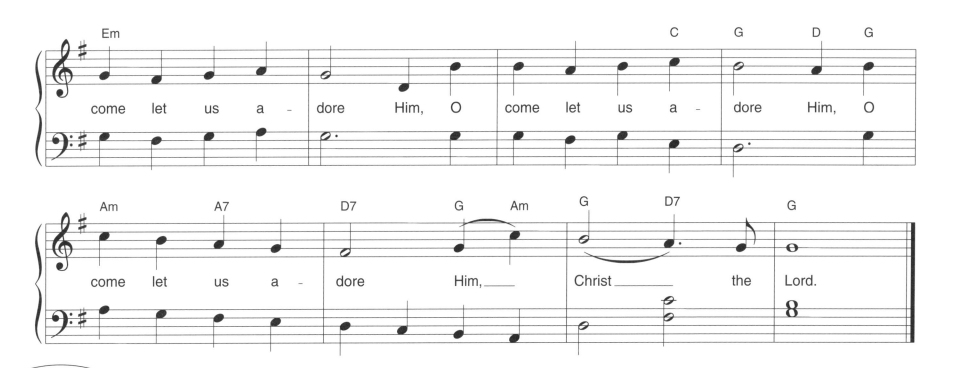

Start the chorus very quietly and sing each line a little louder.

2.
God of God,
Light of Light,
Lo! He abhors not the Virgin's womb;
Very God,
Begotten, not created:

O come let us adore him...

3.
Sing, choir of angels,
Sing in exultation,
Sing, all you citizens of heaven above;
Glory to God
In the highest:

O come let us adore him...

4. Yea, Lord, we greet Thee,
Born this happy morning,
Jesu, to Thee be glory given;
Word of the Father,
Now in flesh appearing:

O come let us adore him...

We Wish You A Merry Christmas

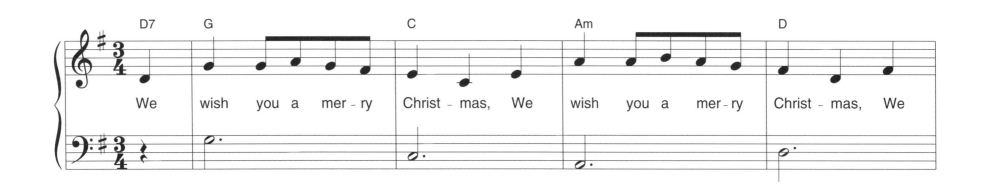

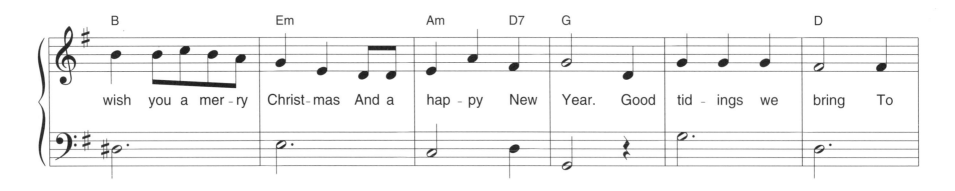

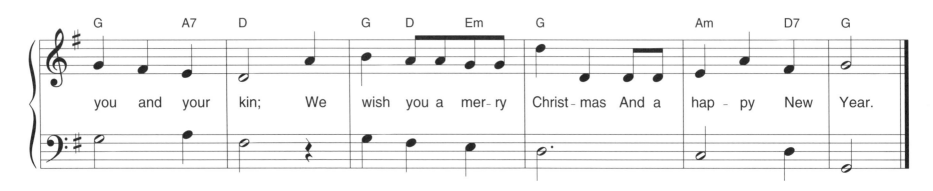

1. We wish you a merry Christmas,
    We wish you a merry Christmas,
    We wish you a merry Christmas
    And a happy new year.

    Good tidings we bring
    To you and your kin;
    We wish you a merry Christmas
    And a happy new year.

2. We all want some figgy pudding,
    We all want some figgy pudding,
    We all want some figgy pudding,
    So bring some right here!

    Good tidings we bring...

3. We won't go until we get some,
    We won't go until we get some,
    We won't go until we get some,
    So bring some right here!

    Good tidings we bring...

Unto Us A Boy Is Born

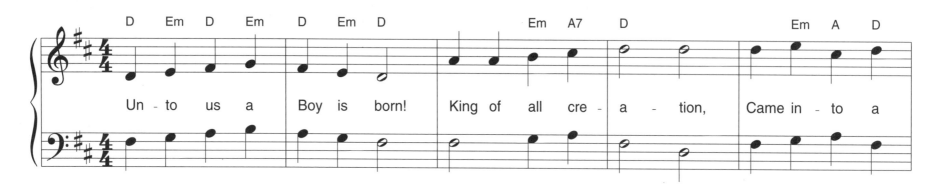

Sing this carol quite slowly.

1. Unto us a Boy is born!
    King of all creation.
    Came into a world forlorn,
    The Lord of every nation.

2. Cradled in a stall was he
    With sleepy cows and asses;
    But the very beasts could see
    That He all men surpasses.

3. Herod then with fear was filled:
    "A prince," he said, "in Jewry!"
    All the little boys he killed
    At Bethlehem in his fury.

4. Now may Mary's Son, who came
    So long ago to love us,
    Lead us all with hearts aflame
    Unto the joys above us.

5. Omega and alpha He!
    Let the organ thunder,
    While the choir with peals of glee,
    Doth rend the air asunder.